1·2·3 BOOKS

Written by Jean Warren

Illustrated by Cora L. Walker

Simple Books To Make For Working With Young Children

Warren Publishing House, Inc.
Everett, Washington

Editor: Gayle Bittinger
Contributing Editor: Elizabeth S. McKinnon
Assistant Editor: Claudia G. Reid
Layout and Cover Design: Kathy Jones
Cover Illustration: Marion Hopping Ekberg

ISBN 0-911019-23-5

Library of Congress Catalog Number 89-050120
Printed in the United States of America
Published by: Warren Publishing House, Inc.
         P.O. Box 2255
         Everett, WA 98203

Introduction

Books occupy a special place in the lives of young children. Some books instill a love of reading and adventure, while others instill a love for discovery and creative expression.

Young children need to be introduced to many different kinds of books. Besides read-aloud story books, they need their own beginning books to "read" and learn from. They need interactive books that call for immediate responses, that encourage language development and that provide opportunities for critical thinking.

1•2•3 BOOKS is a collection of ideas for making the kinds of books that involve and teach young children. You will find directions and patterns on the following pages for creating a variety of easy-to-make, inexpensive books. Each of these beginning books can be tailored to capture your children's special interests and imaginations. And all of the books can be used to enhance your children's thinking and language skills.

Contents

Books

Teddy Bear Book

Materials: Felt squares; felt scraps; needle and thread; glue; pair of scissors.

Making the Book: Cut a bear shape and a pocket shape out of felt scraps. Glue three edges of the pocket shape to a felt square. Put the bear shape inside the pocket (do not glue it). Then set out four additional felt squares. Cut a variety of shapes out of felt scraps to create a different scene for each square. Glue the shapes to the squares. Put the felt squares together with the bear page on top. Sew the felt pages together on the left-hand side.

Using the Book: Let the children take the bear out of the pocket and move it from page to page. (The bear will stick to the felt pages as it would to a flannelboard.) Have them make up a story about what the bear is doing on each page.

Story Picture Book

Materials: Photo album with magnetic pages; magazines; box; clear self-stick paper; pair of scissors.

Making the Book: Cut a variety of pictures out of magazines. Cover the pictures with clear self-stick paper and place them in a box. Ask a child to choose several pictures from the box. Then help the child put the pictures in a magnetic-page photo album in any order.

Using the Book: Let the child "read" the book by making up a story to fit the pictures. To make a new book, have the child replace the old pictures with new ones.

Folding Worm Book

Materials: Large index cards; felt-tip markers; tape.

Making the Book: Fold large index cards in half. Then unfold the cards and tape them together end to end. (Tape both sides of the cards for a more durable book.) Draw the head of a worm on the first half of the first card. Then draw a section of the worm on each of the following card halves. Write a number in each section. Fold the cards together accordion style.

Using the Book: Stand the book on a low shelf or table. Ask the children to identify the number in each section of the worm.

Variation: Instead of writing numbers, attach stickers to the worm sections for counting. Or use felt-tip markers to make each section a different color.

Sticker Story Book

Materials: Clear plastic page covers; magazines; identical stickers of one character such as a teddy bear, a bee or a butterfly; three-ring binder; pair of scissors.

Making the Book: Cut full-page pictures out of magazines. Randomly attach a sticker of the same character to each picture. Slide the pictures, back to back, into clear plastic page covers. Put the pages in a three-ring binder.

Using the Book: Let the children tell a story about the sticker character as it is seen on each page of the book.

Variation: Glue magazine pictures to both sides of pieces of construction paper and attach a character sticker to each picture. Cover the pictures with clear self-stick paper. Then staple the pages together on the left-hand side.

Follow the Bouncing Ball Book

Materials: Wing-type wallet photo holder; magazines; small self-stick circles all one color; pair of scissors.

Making the Book: Cut small pictures out of magazines and trim them to fit in the pages of a wing-type wallet photo holder. Attach a self-stick circle to each picture. Put two of the pictures in each of the pages, picture sides out.

Using the Book: Let the children tell the story of the "bouncing ball" as it moves from page to page.

Rubber Stamp Book

Materials: Large index cards; several rubber stamps (including at least one person or animal character); stamp pad; hole punch; brass paper fasteners.

Making the Book: Put several large index cards together, punch two holes on the left-hand side and insert two brass paper fasteners. Use a rubber stamp of a person or an animal to print that character on each page of the book. Then turn each page into a simple picture by using the other rubber stamps to create scenes.

Using the Book: Let the children take turns "reading" the book by making up a story about the character that appears on each page.

Variation: Give each of the children several index cards and let them stamp on pictures to make their own books. Then have them read their books to you.

Paper Bag Book

Materials: Small paper bags; felt-tip markers; stapler; pair of scissors.

Making the Book: Cut 2 inches off the top of several small paper bags. Place the bags on top of one another with the flaps on the right. Then staple the bags together on the left-hand side to make a book. Use felt-tip markers to draw a picture under each flap so that part of the picture is visible when the flap is closed. If desired, select a theme for the book, such as animals, holidays or circus characters.

Using the Book: As the children look through the book, have them try to guess what is hidden beneath each flap before lifting the flap up.

Variation: Instead of drawing a picture, glue a picture cut from a magazine under each flap.

Mini Movie Book

Materials: Small notepad; felt-tip markers.

Making the Book: Hold a small notepad with the binding on the left. Draw a snowflake (or other simple object) at the top of the first page about 2 inches from the right side. On the second page, draw an identical snowflake slightly down and to the right of where it was on the first page. Continue on each page until the snowflake is at the bottom right-hand corner.

Using the Book: Let the children take turns making the snowflake "fall" by holding the notepad in their left hand and flipping through the pages with their right hand.

Shadow Book

Materials: Magazines; clear self-stick paper; hole punch; black and white construction paper; yarn; pair of scissors.

Making the Book: Cut six medium-sized pictures of familiar objects (or animals) out of magazines. Glue the pictures to black construction paper and trim around the edges of each picture. Cut six 6- by 12-inch rectangles out of clear self-stick paper. Remove the backing from one piece and lay it on a table, sticky side up. Place a picture in the middle of the lower half of the rectangle and fold the top half down over it. Repeat with the remaining pictures. Trim all six picture pages to a uniform size. Cut six pages of the same size out of white construction paper. Put the book together by alternating picture pages (with black sides facing up) and white pages. Punch holes on the left-hand side of the book and tie the pages together with yarn.

Using the Book: As the children look through the pages in the book, have them try to guess what objects are making the black "shadows."

Riddle Book

Materials: Large index cards; felt-tip markers; stapler.

Making the Book: Staple several large index cards together to make a book. On the back of each page, draw a picture of a simple object. On the front of each page, write a two- or three-line riddle describing the object. For example, if you drew a picture of an apple on the back of a page, the front of the page might read: "It grows on a tree. It is a fruit. Sometimes it is red and sometimes it is green or yellow."

Using the Book: Read each riddle to the children and let them try to guess the name of the object before turning the page.

Variation: Instead of drawing objects, cut pictures out of magazines and glue them to the backs of the pages.

Guess What It Is Book

Materials: Clear plastic page cover; typing paper; magazines; brass paper fasteners; hole punch; craft knife; pair of scissors.

Making the Book: Punch three holes down the left-hand side of six sheets of typing paper and put them together with brass paper fasteners. Use a craft knife to cut out a square through all six pages. Fold back the first page and cut out a triangle through the remaining five pages. Repeat, cutting out a circle through pages three to six, a rectangle through pages four to six, a heart through pages five and six and an oval through page six. Attach a clear plastic page cover to the back of the pages. Cut several full-page pictures out of magazines. Insert one of the pictures in the plastic page cover.

Using the Book: Let the children look through the cut-out shapes as they turn each page and have them try to guess what picture will be revealed when all the pages have been turned. Then insert a new picture in the plastic page cover and let them try again.

Color Book

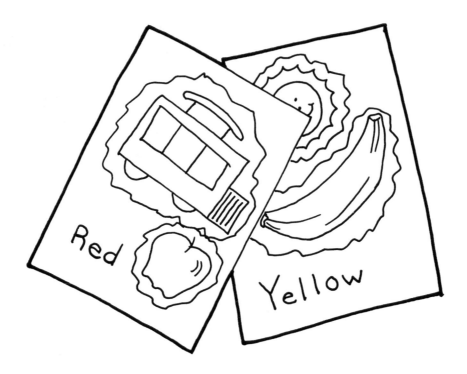

Materials: Magazines; construction paper; felt-tip markers; stapler; glue; pair of scissors.

Making the Book: Select several sheets of different colored construction paper. Cut out two or three matching colored magazine pictures for each color. Use a felt-tip marker to write the name of the color at the bottom of each piece of construction paper. Glue the pictures on the appropriate pages. Staple the pages together to make a book.

Using the Book: Let the children take turns "reading" the color names and naming the items pictured on each page.

Variation: Make a book for just one color, such as red. Cut out several red magazine pictures and glue each one to a separate piece of red construction paper.

Number Book

Materials: Stickers; construction paper; felt-tip markers; stapler.

Making the Book: Number five pieces of construction paper from 1 to 5. Attach a corresponding number of stickers to each page. Staple the pages together on the left-hand side.

Using the Book: Let the children take turns identifying the numbers on the pages and counting the stickers.

Variation: Make a book for just one number, such as "4." Write the number on several sheets of construction paper. Then attach a different set of four stickers to each page, such as four teddy bears, four rainbows, four flowers or four stars.

Shape Book

Materials: Felt-tip markers; stapler; pair of scissors.

Making the Book: Photocopy the following pattern pages. Cut the pages in half and use felt-tip markers to color them as desired. Staple the pages together on the left-hand side.

Using the Book: Let the children try to find the "hidden" shapes on each page.

Sequence Book

Materials: Clear self-stick paper; brass paper fasteners; hole punch; felt-tip markers; pair of scissors.

Making the Book: Photocopy the following pattern pages. Color the pages with felt-tip markers as desired. Then cover the pages with clear self-stick paper for durability. Cut the pages in half, put them together and punch two holes on the left-hand side.

Using the Book: Mix up the pages and let the child put them in sequential order before inserting the brass paper fasteners. To let another child use the book, remove the paper fasteners and again mix up the pages.

Variation: Draw your own pictures of a sequence of events on large index cards. For example, you could draw pictures showing the hatching of a chick (an egg in its nest, the egg cracking, the chick partly out of the shell and the chick completely hatched) or the making of a cake (mixing the ingredients together, pouring the batter into pans, baking the cake, frosting the cake and eating the cake).

SEED

SEED

Butter Cup Nursery

Boat Book

Materials: Stickers; felt-tip markers; stapler; pair of scissors.

Making the Book: Photocopy the following pattern pages. Cut each of the pages in half and put them in numerical order. Staple the pages together on the left-hand side. Attach stickers to the pages as shown above so that boat one has one sticker, boat two has the same sticker as boat one plus another sticker and so on through boat five. Then attach one each of all five stickers to the picture of the capsized boat. Use felt-tip markers to color the pages as desired.

Using the Book: Let the children count the stickers, name the numbers and tell a story about how the boat gets too full and capsizes.

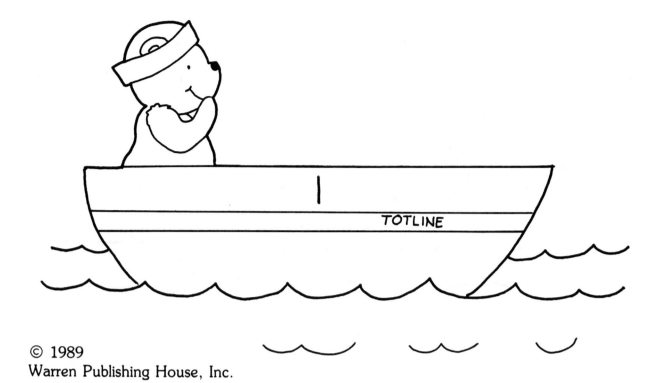

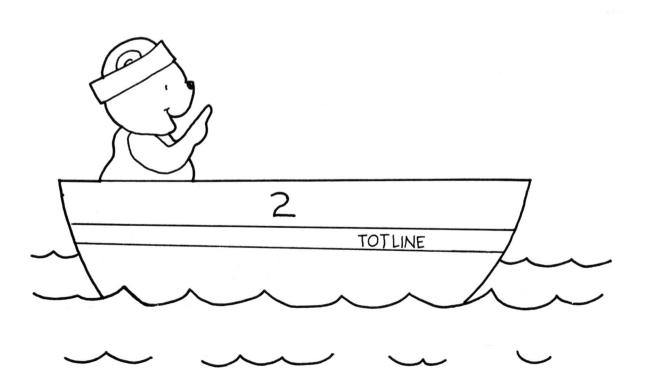

- -

5

What Will I Wear? Book

Materials: Child's photo; felt-tip markers; stapler; glue; craft knife; pair of scissors.

Making the Book: Photocopy the following pattern pages. Glue a photo of a child's face in the dotted section on the last page. Use a craft knife to cut the dotted section out of each of the remaining pages. Put the pages together with the photo page last. Carefully position the pages so that the photo can be seen through each opening. Then staple the pages together on the left-hand side and trim. Color the pages with felt-tip markers as desired.

Using the Book: Let the child look through the book and describe what he or she is wearing on each page.

Variation: If several children will be using the book, make this simple change. Instead of gluing one child's photo to the back page, glue on a clear plastic photo holder so that a different child's photo can be inserted each time.

What will I wear?

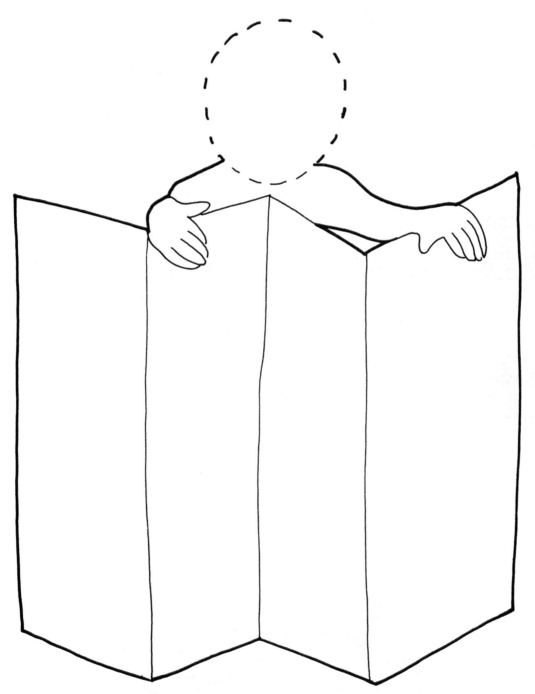

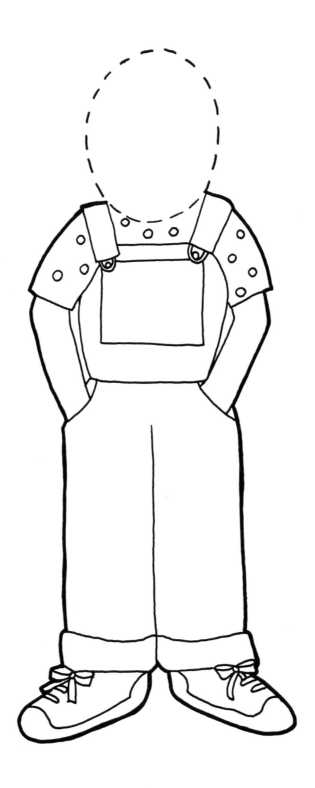

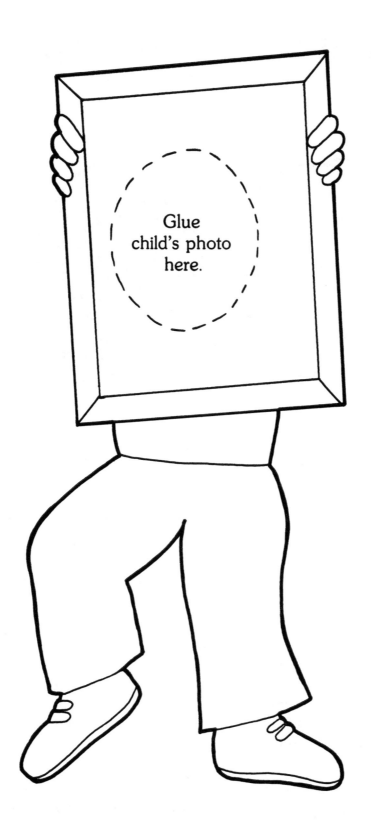

Glue child's photo here.

Weather Wheel Book

Materials: Posterboard; brass paper fastener; craft knife; crayons; glue; pair of scissors.

Making the Book: Photocopy the following pattern pages. Use crayons to color the patterns. Glue the patterns to posterboard and cut them out. Use a craft knife to cut out the dotted sections in the square-shaped patterns. Select one of the square patterns, put it on top of the circle pattern and connect them with a brass paper fastener as indicated by the x's.

Using the Book: Let the children rotate the circle to watch the weather change. Ask them to describe the weather they see in each picture.

Under the Big Top Book

Materials: Clear self-stick paper; felt-tip markers; stapler; pair of scissors.

Making the Book: Photocopy the following pattern pages. Color the patterns with felt-tip markers, then cut them out. Cover each pattern on both sides with 8½- by 11-inch pieces of self-stick paper. Arrange the patterns in a pile so that the smallest picture is on the bottom and is hidden by the next smallest picture and so on until the circus tent picture is on the top. Staple the pages together on the left-hand side and trim them to a uniform size.

Using the Book: Let the children take turns discovering the pictures that are hidden "under the big top."

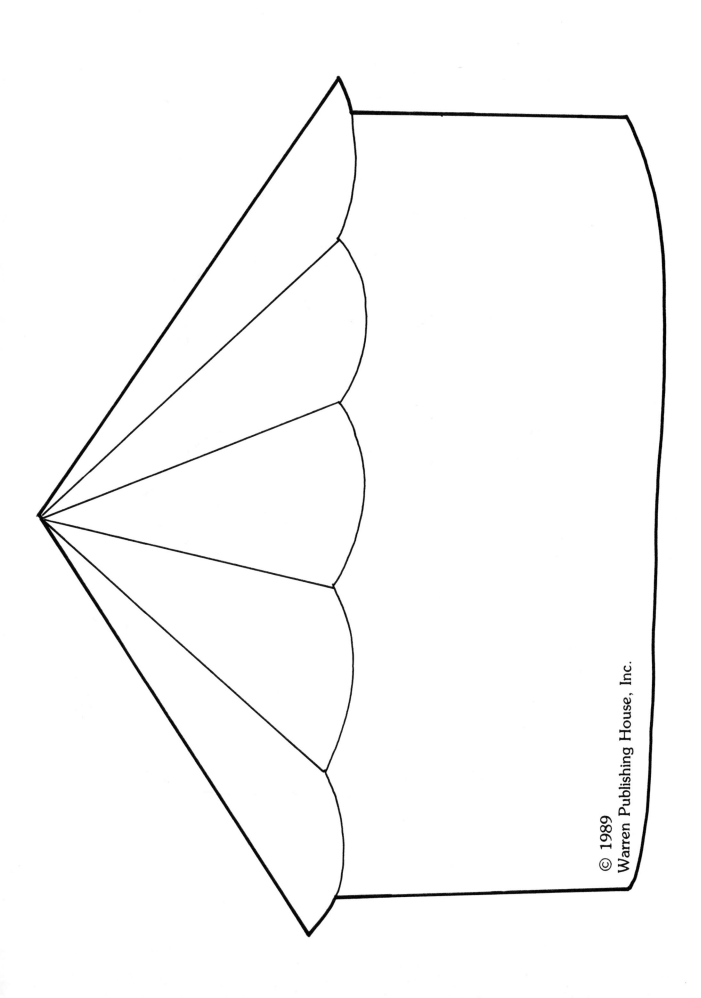

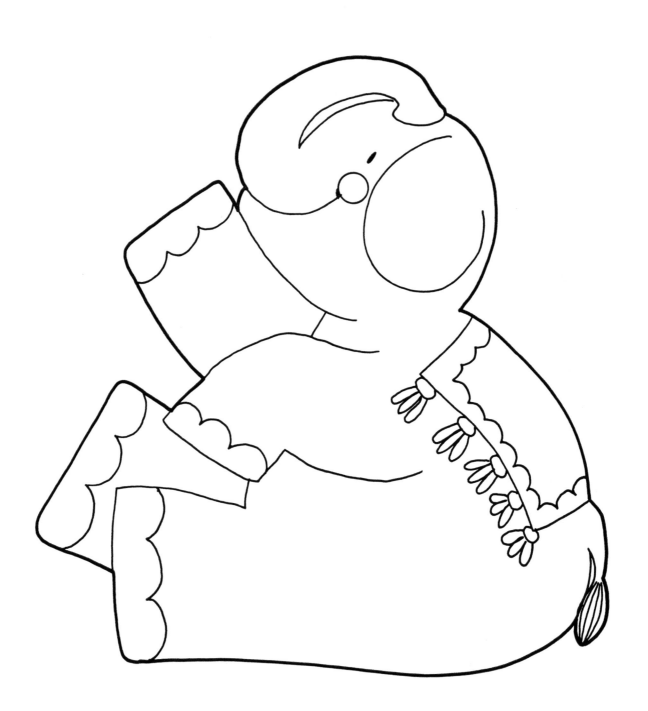

Wheels Book

Materials: Felt-tip markers; stapler; pair of scissors.

Making the Book: Photocopy the following pattern pages. Use felt-tip markers to color each pattern a different color. Cut out the patterns along the dotted lines. Put the patterns together and staple the book across the top.

Using the Book: Let each child "read" the book by naming the colors of the vehicles and telling what the vehicles are used for.

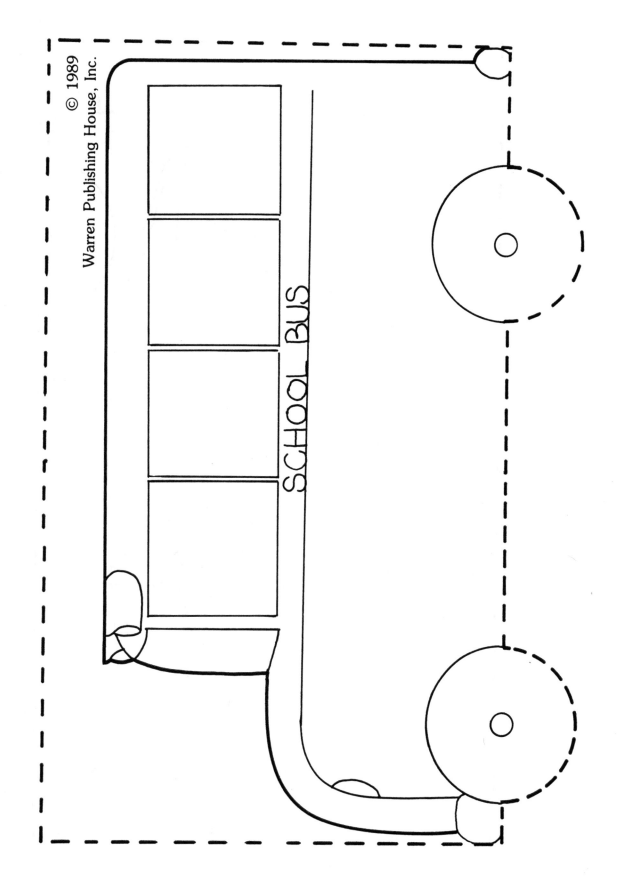

SCHOOL BUS

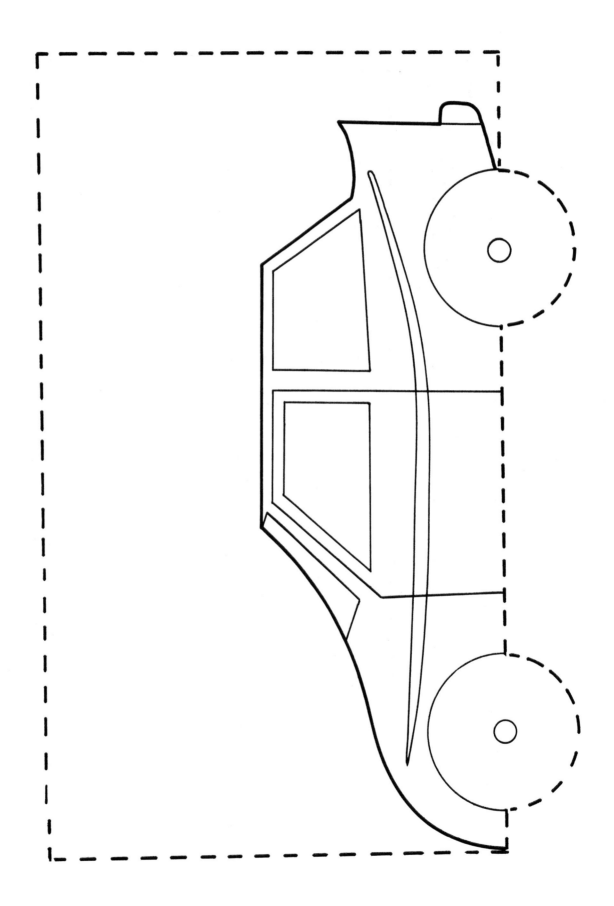

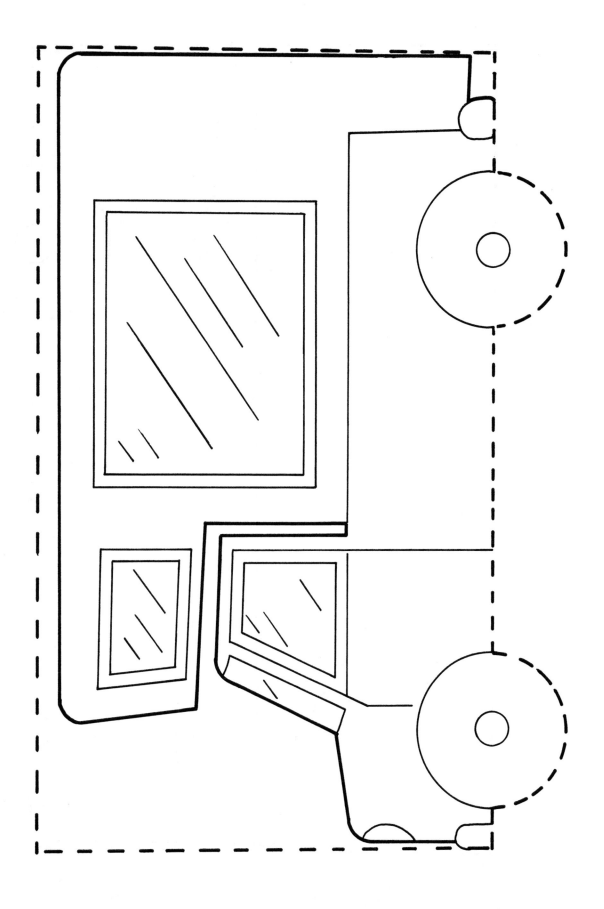

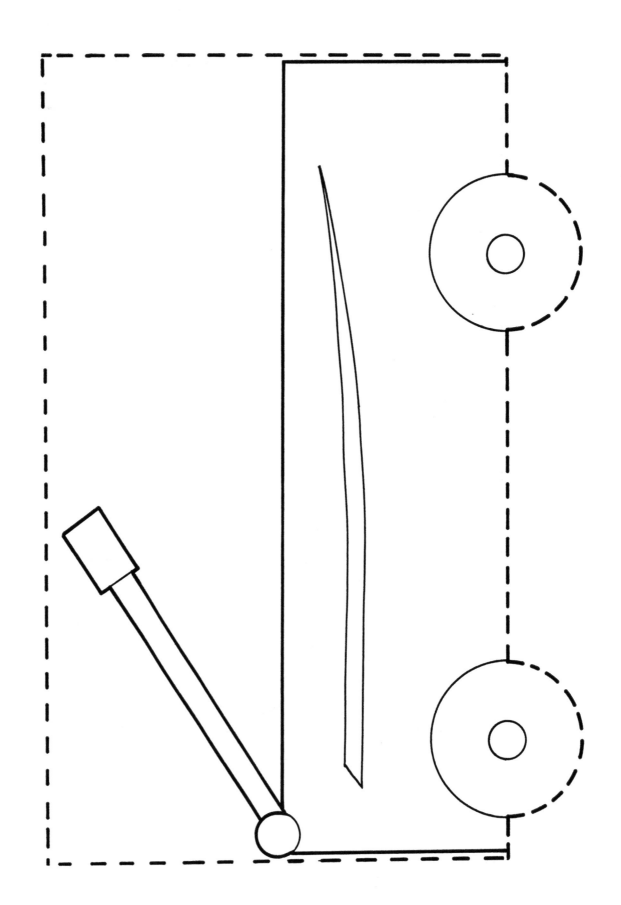

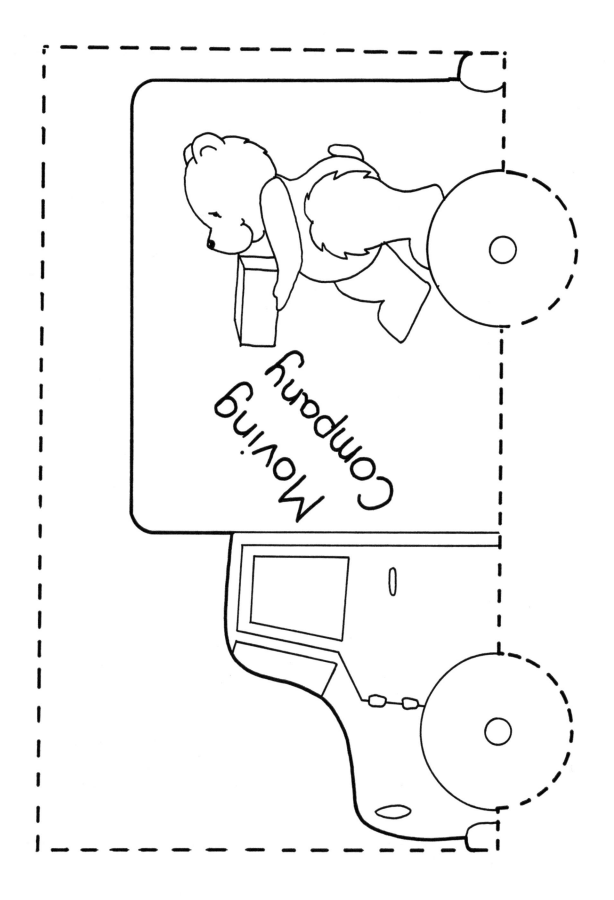

Caterpillar Book

Materials: Posterboard; clear self-stick paper; hole punch; felt-tip markers; yarn; glue; craft knife.

Making the Book: Photocopy the following pattern pages. Glue each page to an 8½- by 11-inch piece of posterboard. Color the pages with felt-tip markers. Then cover them with clear self-stick paper. Use a craft knife to cut a small hole in each page as indicated by the dotted circle. Put the pages together and punch two holes on the left-hand side. Then tie the pages together with yarn.

Using the Book: Draw a face on the end of your finger with a felt-tip marker. Insert your finger through the holes in the pages and let the children take turns making up stories about the "caterpillar."

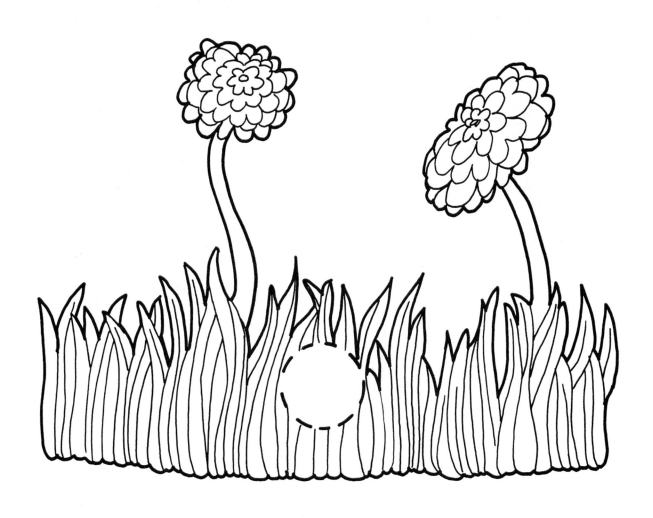

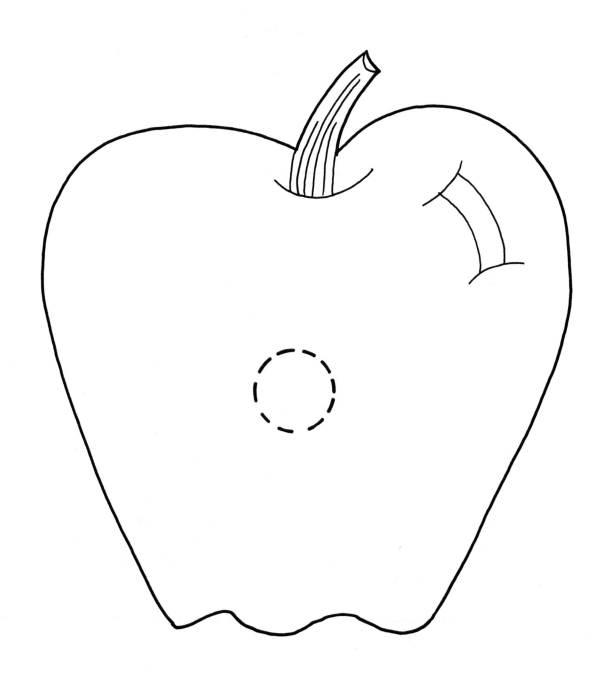

What Will I Be? Book

**What will
I be?**

Materials: Child's photo; felt-tip markers; stapler; glue; pair of scissors.

Making the Book: Photocopy the following pattern pages. Glue a photo of a child's face in the dotted section on the page that reads "For now, I'll just be me." Cut the dotted section out of each of the remaining pages. Put the pages together with the "What will I be?" page first and the page with the child's photo on it last. Carefully position the pages so that the photo can be seen through each opening. Staple the pages together on the left-hand side and trim. Use felt-tip markers to color the pages as desired.

Using the Book: Let the child look through the book and describe what he or she is doing on each page.

Variation: If several children will be using the book, make this simple change. Instead of gluing one child's photo to the back page, glue on a clear plastic photo holder so that a different child's photo can be inserted each time.

What will
I be?

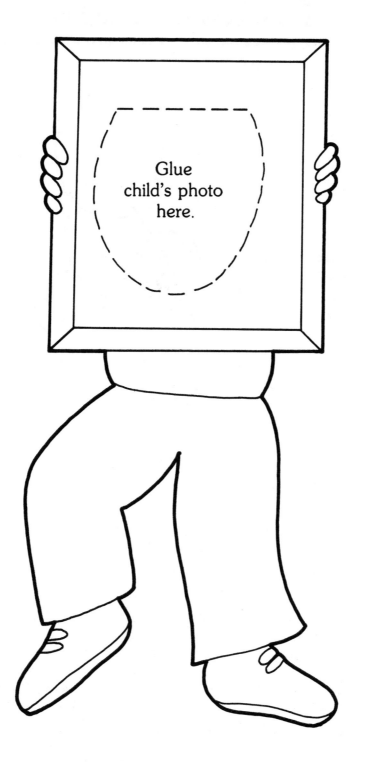

**For now
I'll just be me!**

Texture Book

Materials: Textured materials such as fabric scraps, sandpaper, cotton balls, corrugated cardboard and aluminum foil; hole punch; metal rings; felt-tip markers; glue; pair of scissors.

Making the Book: Photocopy the following pattern pages. Using the small patterns as guides, cut each shape out of a different kind of textured material. Glue each shape to the appropriate pattern pages. Then glue a cotton ball tail to the bunny pattern page. Color the remaining parts of each page with felt-tip markers. Put the pages together and punch two holes on the left-hand side. Then fasten the pages together with metal rings.

Using the Book: Let the children take turns touching the different textures and making up stories about each page.

Activities, songs and new ideas to use right now are waiting for you in every issue of the TOTLINE newsletter.

Each issue puts the fun into teaching with 24 pages of challenging and creative activities for young children, including open-ended art activities, learning games, music, language and science activities.

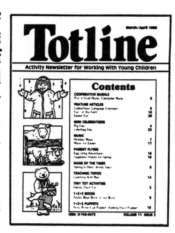

Sample issue $1.00

One year subscription (6 issues) $15.00

Beautiful bulletin boards, games and flannelboards are easy with PRESCHOOL PATTERNS.

You won't want to miss a single issue of PRESCHOOL PATTERNS with 3 large sheets of patterns delightfully and simply drawn. Each issue includes patterns for making flannelboard characters, bulletin boards, learning games and more!

Sample issue $2.00

One year subscription (6 issues) $18.00

ORDER FROM:
Warren Publishing House, Inc. • P.O. Box 2255, Dept. B • Everett, WA 98203

Totline Books

Super Snacks – 120 seasonal sugarless snack recipes kids love.

Teaching Tips – 300 helpful hints for working with young children.

Teaching Toys – over 100 toy and game ideas for teaching learning concepts.

Piggyback Songs – 110 original songs, sung to the tunes of childhood favorites.

More Piggyback Songs – 195 more original songs.

Piggyback Songs for Infants and Toddlers – 160 original songs, for infants and toddlers.

Piggyback Songs in Praise of God – 185 original religious songs, sung to familiar tunes.

Piggyback Songs in Praise of Jesus – 240 more original religious songs.

Holiday Piggyback Songs – over 240 original holiday songs.

1•2•3 Art – over 200 open-ended art activities.

1•2•3 Games – 70 no-lose games for ages 2 to 8.

1•2•3 Colors – over 500 Color Day activities for young children.

1•2•3 Puppets – over 50 puppets to make for working with young children.

1•2•3 Murals – over 50 murals to make with children's open-ended art.

1•2•3 Books – over 20 beginning books to make for working with young children.

Teeny-Tiny Folktales – 15 folktales from around the world plus flannelboard patterns.

Short-Short Stories – 18 original stories plus seasonal activities.

Mini-Mini Musicals – 10 simple musicals, sung to familiar tunes.

Small World Celebrations – 16 holidays from around the world to celebrate with young children.

"Cut & Tell" Scissor Stories for Fall – 8 original stories plus patterns.

"Cut & Tell" Scissor Stories for Fall – 8 original stories plus patterns.

"Cut & Tell" Scissor Stories for Spring – 8 original stories plus patterns.

Seasonal Fun – 50 two-sided reproducible parent flyers.

Theme-A-Saurus – the great big book of mini teaching themes.

Check your local school supply store for these outstanding books or write for our FREE catalog.

Warren Publishing House, Inc. • P.O. Box 2255, Dept. B • Everett, WA 98203